REC'D
FEB 3 1993
1004
FACILITIES PLANNING & MANAGEMENT

COACHING

SELF-DIRECTED WORKTEAMS

BUILDING WINNING TEAMS IN TODAY'S CHANGING WORKPLACE

PETER R. GARBER

ORGANIZATION DESIGN AND DEVELOPMENT, INC.
King of Prussia, Pennslyvania

© 1993 Peter R. Garber.

All rights reserved. No part of this publication may be reproduced, stored in any type of a retrieval system, or transmitted in whole or in part, in any form or by any means, electronic, mechanical, photocopying, recording or otherwise, without the prior written permission of Organization Design and Development, Inc., 2002 Renaissance Boulevard, Suite 100, King of Prussia, Pennsylvania 19406. (215) 279-2002.

Prepared for publication by Organization Design and Development, Inc. Printed in the United States of America.

Library of Congress Catalog Card Number: 92-62476
ISBN: 0-925652-17-2

10   9   8   7   6   5   4   3   2   1

To my wife Nancy and daughters, Lauren and Erin.

CONTENTS

INTRODUCTION vii

PART ONE: SELF-DIRECTED WORKTEAMS 1
  Self-Direction: Confusing at Best 1
  The Team Concept 2
  The Players 4
  You're Not Listening 5

PART TWO: SELF-DIRECTED COACHING 7
  Who's in Charge? 7
  From Boss to Coach 8
  Activity 1: Your Role as a Supervisor 11
  The Missed Field Goal 14
  Activity 2: The Effects of Confidence 15
  Activity 3: The Greatest Coach 17

PART THREE: FROM THE SIDELINES 19
  Activity 4: The Team Owner 21
  Activity 5: The Fans 23
  Activity 6: Community Support 25
  Activity 7: Publicity 27
  Activity 8: Monday Morning Quarterback 29

PART FOUR: BUILDING THE TEAM 31
  Building a Winning Team 31
  Activity 9: Bench Strength 33
  Activity 10: The Basics of the Game 35
  Activity 11: Playbook 37
  Activity 12: Game Plan 39
  Activity 13: Goals 41
  Activity 14: Unsung Heros 43
  Activity 15: The Opponent 45
  Activity 16: Game Films and Scouting Reports 47
  Activity 17: Keeping Score 49
  Activity 18: The Two-Minute Drill 51
  Activity 19: Winning Year 53
  Activity 20: The Super Bowl 55
  Activity 21: Rebuilding Year 57

PART FIVE: COACHING A WINNING TEAM 59

   Activity 22: Winning Attitude 61

   Activity 23: The Walls.. 63

   Activity 24: We vs. They 65

   Activity 25: Moving in the Same Direction 67

   Activity 26: Out of the Bleachers and onto the Field......................... 69

   Activity 27: What Can I Do about It?... 71

   Activity 28: Ownership.. 73

   Activity 29: Superstars 75

   Activity 30: Work vs. Play.. 77

   Activity 31: The Locker Room 79

PART SIX: GAME PLAY 81

   Activity 32: The Huddle.. 83

   Activity 33: The Defense... 85

   Activity 34: The Offense 86

      • Getting Ready to Play.. 88

      • Play Action 90

   Activity 35: Fumbles/Turnovers.. 95

   Activity 36: The Wrong Call 97

   Activity 37: Penalties 99

   Activity 38: Injuries 101

   Activity 39: Victory Celebrations 103

   Everyone a Champion...104

   Instant Replay 105

PART SEVEN: POST GAME REPORT 107

INTRODUCTION

Coaching Self-Directed Workteams focuses on the new and changing roles of today's supervisors and others in leadership positions, as organizations move toward the concept of self-directed workteams. Often it is helpful to look at our jobs, responsibilities, and roles in life from a new or different perspective. Many times using analogies and examples from other activities with which we are familiar helps to shed new light on the tasks we face on a daily basis. *Coaching Self-Directed Workteams* draws a comparison between the job of a supervisor in today's work environment with that of the coach of a professional football team.

As you read through the content and work through the exercises in this book, imagine that you are the head coach of your favorite team, and your job is to lead that team to the championship. Just as it is with sports, you cannot accomplish that task by yourself. You will need the help, talent, and support of many other people — most importantly, the players on your team. *Coaching Self-Directed Workteams* helps you to look at your job in a variety of ways that can prepare you to motivate your team to reach its greatest potential.

PART ONE

SELF-DIRECTED WORKTEAMS

Self-Direction: Confusing at Best

The concept of self-directed workteams can be confusing and often raises many questions. For example: Who "self-directs" this workteam? What role will each person who is currently in the organization play in the future? As the interest in self-directed workteams becomes more wide-spread in our organizations, these and many other questions must be answered.

The term "self-directed" could be substituted for many similar names currently being used to describe this concept, such as "high-performance," "self-motivated," or "self-managing." Self-direction usually describes a new approach or management style that allows employees more involvement and decision-making responsibility in their jobs. If you have introduced more employee involvement in decision-making in your organization, you know that this concept is not only confusing at first but can be threatening as well. First-line supervisors, middle managers, and even top management are cautious because this concept represents a major change in management philosophy. Self-directed workteams change what everyone is familiar and comfortable with, and any change is difficult, especially when you begin to address lines of authority and the way decisions are made in an organization. However, just as organizations must change, so must their supervisors and managers change.

Change does not always mean that everything will be different. Often we find that the changes that occur in our lives are not totally new concepts but are familiar ones presented to us in a different way. *Coaching Self-Directed Workteams* applies concepts of effective leadership that are used in the sports world to your role as a supervisor in the workplace. Both the coach and the supervisor play similar roles and share many of the same goals and responsibilities. The supervisor of today has as much influence on the success of his or her team of workers as the coach has on his or her team of players. The desired end result of either role is the same — that the "players" reach their highest potential and that the "team" be successful in meeting the expectations and requirements of the organization that supports them.

In every sense of the word, a group of people working together as part of an organization, corporation, or business is as much of a team as any group of people in the sports arena, whether amateur or professional.

The Team Concept

The team concept is *everything* in football. A football team could not function much less be a winner without believing in that concept. What happens when a football team does not play as a team? What would happen if the quarter-back never gave the ball to his teammates and tried to make every yard by himself? Suppose the players stopped blocking for one another? Working together to move the team forward toward the goal is the mission of each player in any football organization — from Little League to the NFL.

Being a member of a self-directed workteam is similar in many ways to playing team sports. Both require working as a team player and contributing to the overall efforts of the group. Both involve supporting other members of the team so that *they* may better perform *their* jobs. Both require hard work, dedication, and commitment if they are to become winners. Both involve people working together to reach shared goals for success. In football the purpose of the game is to score more points than the competition. For self-directed work-teams the goal is the same — to beat the competition. To accomplish this means that each member of the team must share his or her abilities, experiences, and knowledge to help the team win. In order to achieve this goal, all players must feel like a part of the team and perform their jobs to the best of their ability.

Self-directed workteams represent a new approach to the way organizations are managed. In these teams the focus is on the team members themselves, rather than management or supervision, as the driving force for the success of the team and ultimately the entire organization. Regardless of the activity, being a member of a self-directed team requires a total commitment to being the very best you can be.

Oddly enough, in the present world of work, the team concept is not nearly as well-defined or accepted as in the sports world. Organizations are just now beginning to realize the importance of the team concept to their success. In the past, work groups within an organization basically had their own goals and work environment in which they functioned. Groups seldom considered the need to involve members from different levels of the organization to help them reach their goals. Figure 1 shows this traditional organization structure, which has little or minimal interaction among the different levels within the organization.

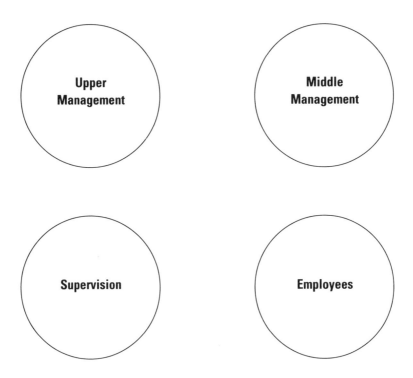

Fig. 1. The traditional organization structure.

Figure 2 illustrates the workteam concept, with the various groups beginning to work together, resulting in increased interaction among the groups. This sets the stage for the "team" concept in the organization.

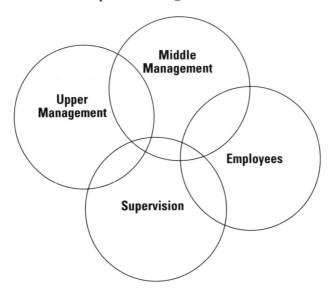

Fig. 2. The workteam concept.

The self-directed workteam concept involves breaking down many of the traditional organization structures that inhibit different groups of individuals from working together or even communicating with one another. Figure 3 depicts the ultimate team concept with people at all levels of the organization working together — sharing their experiences and abilities in order to reach the goals of both the individual and the organization.

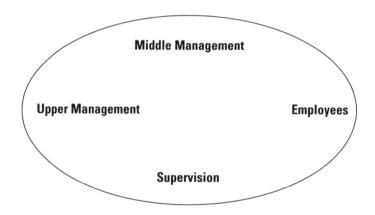

Fig. 3. The team concept.

Try to imagine what it would be like if no one helped anyone else at work? Suppose everyone only worried about his or her own problems and never offered to help co-workers.What would happen if everyone refused to work as a team to solve problems or share ideas or experiences? And suppose each person was just out for himself or herself and didn't care about what happened to anyone else in the organization.

No team — either in sports or in an organization — could ever expect to beat the competition without applying teamwork!

The Players

Self-directed workteams should not be limited just to specific groups, such as hourly employees who traditionally have had little or no decision-making opportunities or involvement in how the organization functions. To be effective in an organization, self-directed workteams can and should be utilized at all levels. Regardless of an employee's position within the organization, each individual needs opportunities to share his or her experiences and knowledge concerning the job. At one time or another most of us have had the experience of helplessly watching mistakes being made by those in higher positions, while we had little or no opportunity to help prevent those mistakes from occurring

— even though we had the knowledge or ability to do so. The concept that those who work closest to the problems or areas in need of improvement are in the best position to make a decision concerning the solution is true for all levels of the organization — including the lowest levels.

You're Not Listening

In the past, managers and supervisors told those who worked for them what jobs to perform and how to perform them. Then they followed-up to ensure that each employee completed his or her work. Typically communication was limited between the boss and the employee regarding exactly how the work was to be completed — the boss gave the orders, the employee did the work. This relationship is changed with the introduction of self-directed workteams.

Self-directed workteams provide everyone with the opportunity to share in the responsibility for knowing what work needs to be completed and for ensuring that it is accomplished in a quality manner. Why this change? It goes back to the concept just stated: those who actually do the work are in the best position to know what work needs to be done, how that work can be performed in a more efficient manner, and how to solve problems that arise regarding that work.

There is a story about an employee who, shortly after the introduction of self-directed workteams in her workplace, made a super, cost-savings suggestion, which the company immediately implemented. Her supervisor said to her: "That was really a great idea. I only wish you had thought of it a long time ago. It sure would have saved us a lot of hassle and expense around here over the years." To this comment the employee replied: "I *did* think of it years ago, and I've been trying to tell you about it all this time. You just haven't listened to me until now!"

Self-directed workteams can help improve communication throughout the organization and provide all employees a greater opportunity to share their ideas of how their jobs and the organization can be improved. A comment such as, "I feel like someone is finally listening to me," is a sure sign that self-directed workteams are succeeding in an organization.

Self-directed workteams are proving that all the knowledge in an organization is not necessarily at the top. Answers and suggestions often come from surprising places. Employees on all levels of organizations are finding answers to problems that have eluded the "traditional experts" for years.

PART TWO

Who's in Charge?

You might ask: "If *everyone* in the organization is going to be making the decisions, who's going to be in charge?" No one would want to sail on a ship without a captain at the helm or play on a team without a coach to lead the way. The same is true when it comes to managing an organization. There will always be a need for supervision in an organization, and management can never give up its responsibility to manage the organization. What *is* changing are the *roles* that management and supervision will play in the future. Many of these changes involve a concept called *empowerment*. Empowerment means giving more people more responsibility and authority, which many managers and supervisors are reluctant to do for a variety of reasons. However, giving more responsibility and authority to others in your organization does not mean that you lose your own. In fact, in many ways the more responsibility and authority you give to others, the more you empower those who work for you, the more you will get in return. When you think about it, you actually are *expanding* your authority by extending your "reach." Instead of two eyes, ears, and hands, you can have as many as those you have empowered to help you in your work.

Concepts such as self-directed workteams mean that employees at all levels of the organization become more involved in "calling the plays." How many times have employees tried to warn management of an "incoming linebacker about to crash through the offensive line to sack the quarterback," which perhaps only they were in a position to see? Typically, management has not listened to this input from employees at lower levels in the organization. Instead management has played on, confident as the "Captain of the Titanic" that they knew all they needed to know about what lay ahead.

Self-directed workteams provide all employees with opportunities to share what they know with the team. Each individual's input is essential to the total success of the team. Each person must be given the chance to be heard if the team expects to be a winner in the highly competitive game. Finding better solutions to problems is only one of the advantages to be gained from letting those closest to the work make the decisions regarding the work. By being involved they also will have a greater sense of commitment, ownership, and pride in that which they have helped to create.

What must you do to set the stage and create the climate for increased involvement and input from employees? This dramatic change will not happen by itself and it will not occur overnight. You need leaders who understand the concepts of self-directed workteams. You need leaders who respect the knowledge, ability, and capability of all of their employees and who empower them to assume greater responsibility in their jobs and to make decisions that affect the entire organization.

Equally important is understanding what self-directed workteams are not. For example, self-directed workteams are *not*:

- just an excuse to reduce the number of supervisory and management personnel.

- simply a way to eliminate the supervisory layer in the organization, while trying to manage as before, except with the decisions being made by the next level above.

- just the new buzzword in business, soon to be replaced by the next management fad to come along. The terminology may change in the future, but the concept will prevail. It will prevail because giving employees greater opportunity to utilize their knowledge, abilities, and talents to the benefit of both the employee and the organization is not only good business — it's the right thing to do!

Self-directed workteams cannot be like a new "toy" that management buys, never replaces the batteries, and later wonders why the toy no longer works. These workteams require constant attention and nurturing in order to be successful. Self-directed workteams need the support of everyone, at all levels of the organization, on a regular and ongoing basis.

From Boss to Coach

Of all the changes that come with self-directed workteams, the new role of the supervisor is perhaps the greatest challenge. Having self-directed workteams does not mean that the role of the supervisor is eliminated, or even diminished — it is enlarged. Nor does it mean simply giving more work to supervisors — they already have enough to do. It means changing the traditional supervisory role to that of a coach who develops the potential of all the team members.

To put the impact of this change into perspective, the following is a brief look at some of the traditional responsibilities and the new responsibilities of both the supervisor and the employee.

Traditional Responsibilities

Supervisor

Assigns jobs
Sets schedules
Prepares plans
Obtains supplies/equipment
Makes adjustments
Makes corrections
Monitors quality assurance
Performs operation maintenance
Prepares production reports
Performs safety inspections
Etc.

Employee

Performs tasks of the job
   assigned by the supervisor

New Responsibilities

Supervisor

Coaching
Coordinating
Supporting
Enabling
Training
Clarifying
Listening
Planning
Delegating
Reinforcing
Communicating
Etc.

Employee

Assigns jobs
Sets schedules
Plans work
Places orders
Makes adjustments
Makes corrections
Monitors quality assurance
Performs operation maintenance
Prepares production reports
Performs safety inspections
Performs other tasks as needed;
   is self-directed

Obviously, the roles of both positions are changing as employees accept more of the responsibilities of the traditional supervisor. Spend a few minutes now and respond to Activity 1.

ACTIVITY 1

The following questions will help you to analyze your own role as a supervisor.

1. As was stated earlier, employees want and are able to accept increased responsibility in their jobs. And no one knows more about what should or could be done about those jobs than the people who actually are doing the work. As a supervisor, ask yourself this question: "How much of *your* time do you spend answering the questions to which your employees already know the answer? What is the nature of some of those questions?

    _____

    _____

    _____

    _____

    _____

    If your response is that you spend a considerable amount of time answering those kinds of questions from your employees, it is likely that you have never empowered them with the responsibility for making those kinds of decisions.

2. Now ask yourself this question: "What could you do in your role as a supervisor that would move your group/crew/shift/department/ organization toward reaching and exceeding the goals you have for your team?" List as many ideas as you can.

    _____

    _____

    _____

    _____

    _____

    _____

    _____

    _____

11

3. How many of the activities listed in #2 are you presently doing on a daily basis? List them below.

_____

_____

_____

_____

_____

_____

_____

4. How similar was your list of what you "could do" to the list of what you "actually do" daily? How do the traditional responsibilities of the supervisor get in the way of your effectiveness in moving your organization toward reaching your goals? If you were not able to list all or even a few of the "could do" activities on your "daily activities" list, why is that the case?

_____

_____

_____

_____

_____

_____

_____

_____

_____

_____

Most likely, if you are not able to accomplish the critical tasks you listed, it is because you do not have the time — because you are wrapped up in the traditional responsibilities of a supervisor. Why not try using self-directed workteams to help you? Instead of running around "putting out fires" and trying to solve all of the problems yourself, prevent the problems in the first place by empowering your employees to take on those responsibilities. Allow them to use their talents and abilities to assume more responsible roles, which will allow *you* to focus on your new role — one that is critical to the organization's success.

Earlier it was said that the concept of self-directed workteams comes in many different forms and is known by many different names. Consequently, one of the most difficult aspects of adapting to a self-directed workteam philosophy is defining exactly what it is. There are no clear-cut requirements or formats for you to follow, rather there are any number of variations of such workteams. Regardless of the label it is given, the most important aspect of any self-directed approach is the involvement and participation of all employees in making decisions and accepting responsibility for what is occuring in their workplace.

In summary, there will always be a need and an important role for supervisors as organizations move toward utilizing self-directed workteams. However, those roles and responsibilities are rapidly changing. They are becoming more important than ever before and are having a greater impact on the entire organization. The supervisor's role is that of becoming more of a manager or coach than that of a boss. In this new work configuration, supervisors must spend their time developing the talents of the people working for them and allow everyone to have a job that is more challenging, productive, and meaningful.

The Missed Field Goal

During an important collegiate football game between two teams, each fighting for national recognition as the number one team in the country, a young place kicker missed a critical field goal that should have been easy to make. It came late in the third quarter, and if he had made it, it would have put his team ahead. The home-field crowd hushed in disappointment as it watched the soaring end-over-end football lose momentum and veer off to the left, missing the uprights by just inches. The kicker slowly walked back to the sidelines, looking at the ground as though ashamed and afraid to face his teammates and most of all the coach because he had let them down when they needed him most. At that moment, he looked like the loneliest person in the world.

However, instead of ignoring him or telling him what he did wrong, or worse yet, yelling at him, the coach stopped what he was doing, walked over to the kicker, placed his hands on each side of his helmet, looked the young man in the eyes and said: "You are a great place kicker and don't forget it! You know as well as I do that you are not going to make every kick. The game is not over and there will be other opportunities. You are not the only one responsible for where we are right now. We are a team, and everyone contributes to what happens to us, either good or bad. I believe in you or you wouldn't be out here today. But most important, don't *you* quit believing in yourself!" Seeing their coach's actions, the rest of the players followed his lead and greeted the place kicker at the bench as though he had made the field goal.

In the final seconds of the game, the place kicker once again was called on to perform. He kicked the longest field goal of his career, helping his team to win the game by one point and become the national champions.

Why do you think this story has been repeated here? Turn now to the following pages and respond to the questions in Activity 2 and Activity 3.

ACTIVITY 2

THE EFFECTS OF CONFIDENCE

1. Do you believe the coach's actions or those of the rest of the team had anything to do with the the place kicker making that last field goal? If so, what affect do you think each had?

    _____

    _____

    _____

    _____

    _____

    _____

    Confidence in your employees' capabilities, as well as their ability to make important decisions concerning their work, is essential to the success of self-directed workteams.

2. What affect might showing trust and confidence in the members of your team have on their performance?

    _____

    _____

    _____

    _____

    _____

    What affect might it have on your own performance?

    _____

    _____

    _____

    _____

    _____

ACTIVITY 3

THE GREATEST COACH

What does it take to be a great coach? Why do some coaches have winning teams year after year, while other coaches produce a win only occasionally? To answer these questions, think about some of the great coaches you have heard of or known.   What were some of the factors that helped them to achieve the level of success they reached?

1. List the skills, traits, abilities, qualities, etc., that you think made these people great coaches.

_____

_____

_____

_____

_____

_____

_____

_____

2. Which of the above characteristics do you think would be effective in dealing with self-directed workteams? Why?

_____

_____

_____

_____

_____

_____

_____

_____

3. Does the coach make the team great, or does the team make the coach great? Why?

_____

_____

_____

_____

_____

_____

_____

_____

PART THREE

All the efforts and actions that lead a team to victory do not necessarily occur on the playing field. There are many other players who do not suit up for the game but who provide essential support for the team, and without whom the team could not exist. They include: the team's owner, the fans, the community in which the team lives, as well as the local media.

In this section, we will review the roles these people play in providing this support from the sidelines for both football teams and self-directed workteams.

ACTIVITY 4

THE TEAM OWNER

In professional sports there is always a team owner, and it is his or her financial investment that supports the team. In some cases the owner may be personally involved in the day-to-day activities of the team. Other owners may only show up on game day or not at all. Regardless, the owner has the authority to make the final decision on any matters concerning the team. Why is it that when a team wins a championship, the owner gets the credit, but when the team loses, it is the coach who gets all the blame?

For any team, support from the top of the organization is essential for its success. The coach of a team wants to keep those at the top of the organization happy and feeling good about the team and wanting to renew his contract each year! How does the coach achieve this goal? By giving the owner what he or she wants — a winning team!

One of the benefits of self-directed workteams is that they provide everyone on the team with a greater sense of ownership and a commitment to be winners. In football winning is easily measured by looking at the team's win/lose record. However, in the workplace winning or losing is not always so easily measured.

1. Who is the "owner" of your team? It may be the company or corporation, the organization, the governmental agency, or private individual who owns or has the overall responsibility for your place of work. What role does the owner play in the success of your team?

   _____

   _____

   _____

   _____

   _____

   _____

   _____

   _____

   _____

   _____

2. What are some of the measures for winning for your team at work?

_____

_____

_____

_____

3. What are the rewards for your team of meeting those measures for winning?

_____

_____

_____

_____

4. What are the consequences of not meeting those measures?

_____

_____

_____

_____

5. What support do you need from your "team owner" for self-directed work-teams to be successful at your place of work?

_____

_____

_____

_____

_____

_____

_____

_____

_____

ACTIVITY 5

A football team's fans are its customers. Fans support the team, pay for the salaries, and are the reason why the team exists. In sports the fans strongest support for their team is when it is winning. But what happens when the team begins to lose? Often only the most loyal fans continue to support a losing team, and even they have their moments of doubt!

In companies the customers are the fans, and they show their support by buying products or services just as fans purchase tickets for a game. However, this support will only continue if the customers receive what they want.

What are the requirements that your team must meet in order to keep the support of your fans/customers?

_____

_____

_____

_____

_____

_____

_____

_____

_____

_____

_____

_____

_____

_____

_____

_____

_____

_____

_____

_____

ACTIVITY 6

For any team the support of the community is essential for its success. The community provides a team with its fans, publicity, practice facilities, and playing field as well as the members' homes. For a business or organization these same critical elements are necessary for success. Your team needs the support of the community in which the members live. In winning as well as in losing seasons the community provides support for a sports team, cheering it on each play of every game, hoping the team will bring home the championship. The entire community shares in each of the team's victories as well as in its defeats. Likewise, the community is an important part of the success of your organization's team, providing the land, utilities, suppliers, services, materials, labor, and other resources essential for the organization to exist and operate.

In turn your business, service, or organization's successes help support the community's families, schools, government, public programs, highways, etc., as well as supporting other businesses in the area.

How can your team and the community in which you live better support each other? How can your team help ensure that you keep the "homefield" advantage in the community in which you live, not only today but in the future as well?

_____

_____

_____

_____

_____

_____

_____

_____

_____

_____

_____

_____

_____

_____

25

ACTIVITY 7

PUBLICITY

Sports teams usually receive a great deal of publicity through the various media, such as newspapers, magazines, television, and radio. The media often closely follows every aspect of a team and its players. This media attention can help provide support for the team and individual players.

This same kind of attention is important to business workteams. Most people appreciate seeing their work publicized in a positive way. They look forward to having their accomplishments recognized and shared with others and often work hard toward that end.

1. What kind of media attention is available for your team? (Some possible sources are company newsletters, bulletin board notices, video and slide presentations, and letters to local community newspapers.)

    _____

    _____

    _____

    _____

    _____

2. How can you make better use of the available publicity resources to help your team?

    _____

    _____

    _____

    _____

    _____

    _____

    _____

    _____

    _____

    _____

ACTIVITY 8

MONDAY MORNING QUARTERBACK

Monday Morning Quarterbacks are those people who, after the game is over, have all the right answers about what should have been done for the team to have played better, regardless of the final results. Like hindsight, a Monday Morning Quarterback's vision is always 20/20 because it is always seen after the fact.

For a few moments you have permission to play Monday Morning Quarterback concerning your place of work. With the benefit of hindsight, what can be done in the future to prevent the mistakes or problems that occurred in the past?

Mistake/Problem	Your Solution

Additional Problems/Solutions

PART FOUR

BUILDING THE TEAM

Building a Winning Team

Imagine that your workgroup is a football team and you are the head coach. How would you begin building your team? Who would be on your starting line-up? Who would play on the frontline and who would be in the backfield? Who would be best suited to be defensive players and who would play on your special teams? Who should play quarterback and who would you depend on to score the extra points?

Now take this fantasy even further. This football team is unlike any found in the NFL. This is a self-directed football team and you are the coach. Imagine that on your self-directed football team the players share in the responsibility of every position. One of the ways that you as head coach can facilitate this sharing is by rotation of job assignments. However, if you are going to rotate assignments, each player must fully understand the responsibilities and requirements of each assignment. To be able to perform more than one position, training must be provided for each role the team members will play. Decisions must be made concerning how often this rotation will occur and the order of this rotation.

By now you may be asking yourself, "Would I really want my tackle playing quarterback or my quarterback playing on the offensive line?" Probably not. However, ask yourself these questions: "How much more appreciation would your quarterback have for what it takes to open up those holes in the defensive line or to provide pass protection after he has played as a tackle for a few games? How much more would the tackle understand about what it is like to have oversized linebackers crashing through the line headed for the quarter-back, if he has had an opportunity to experience that same situation? And how much more knowledgeable and versatile would your players be after learning the skills required for one anothers' roles on the team?

In football everyone looks to the coach to provide the direction for the team. However, does the coach have to call every play? Many of the most successful coaches have empowered their quarterbacks to call their own plays. They believe that their players are in the best position to make these important deci-sions. On your self-directed team, who should call the plays — the coach, the quarterback, the team members? For many of the questions surrounding self-directed workteams, there are no clear-cut or right or wrong answers. However, ask yourself this: "If I am trying to achieve the highest level of commitment and involvement from my team, what would be the best method for calling the plays?" Turn now to the following pages and complete Activities 9 through 21.

ACTIVITY 9

BENCH STRENGTH

A football team must have players who can move into positions that may open up because of injuries, retirements, or players leaving the team. These players must be prepared in advance for stepping into the vacated positions when they occur. In sports a team's ability to replace its starting lineup is referred to as its *bench strength*.

What is your team's bench strength? Have you trained your players for future jobs they may have to fulfill? If not, what needs to be done to help your team acquire the bench strength it needs?

_____

_____

_____

_____

_____

_____

_____

_____

_____

_____

_____

_____

_____

_____

_____

_____

_____

_____

_____

_____

_____

_____

ACTIVITY 10

THE BASICS OF THE GAME

Practice, practice, and more practice. As with anything in life, learning and practicing the basics of the game are essential to success today and for the future. In football these basic skills include blocking, tackling, throwing, catching, physical conditioning, learning the plays, and much more. In today's rapidly changing business world, the skill needed most for the future will be the ability to learn new jobs quickly. What are the basic skills your team players need to do their jobs, not only for today but in the future?

1. List as many skills as you can think of that your employees need in order to perform their jobs today.

_____

_____

_____

_____

_____

_____

_____

_____

_____

2. What skills will be required to work as part of a self-directed workteam in your organization in the future?

_____

_____

_____

_____

_____

_____

_____

_____

3. What steps need to be taken today to help your employees acquire the skills you have identified as being needed in the future (refer to question 2)?

ACTIVITY 11

PLAYBOOK

Every football team needs to have a playbook. A playbook allows each player to know what his exact job assignment is and what his responsibilities are for each play. A football team has a variety of plays that it develops and practices to ensure that it has the ability and flexibility to deal with the ever changing defenses it faces. A well-executed offensive play can defeat even the strongest of defenses.

Your team also needs to have a "playbook" to promote a clear understanding of everyone's job assignments and responsibilities.

1.   How can your team develop its own playbook?

_____

_____

_____

_____

_____

2.   What would that playbook include?

_____

_____

_____

_____

_____

_____

_____

_____

_____

_____

_____

_____

ACTIVITY 12

GAME PLAN

A football team needs to have a game plan that is designed to lead the team to victory. This plan must maximize the strengths and minimize the weaknesses of each player and of the team as a whole. A team's game plan must be modified and adapted to the capabilities of the different competitors it faces each week. Does your team have a game plan?

1. Who should be involved in developing your team's game plan?

    _____
    _____
    _____
    _____
    _____
    _____
    _____

2. How should the team's game plan be communicated?

    _____
    _____
    _____
    _____
    _____
    _____
    _____
    _____
    _____
    _____
    _____

3. How can developing and communicating a game plan help your team reach its goals?

_____

_____

_____

_____

_____

_____

_____

_____

_____

ACTIVITY 13

GOALS

A football team strives to reach its goal line to make touchdowns. The offensive team directs all its efforts toward reaching this single objective. You could say that scoring points is the team's immediate or *short-term goal*, and the *longer-term goal* is winning the game being played. The team's *long-range goal* would be to win the championship or Super Bowl.

1. What are your team's *short-term* goals?

    _____

    _____

    _____

    _____

    _____

2. What are your team's *longer-term* goals?

    _____

    _____

    _____

    _____

    _____

    _____

3. What are your team's *long-range* goals?

    _____

    _____

    _____

    _____

    _____

    _____

ACTIVITY 14

UNSUNG HEROES

A team consists of many individuals working together toward their common goal of being winners. The success of the team, rather than that of the individual players, is most important. Each player's contributions are critical to the team's ultimate success. Each player must perform the responsibilities of his/her position to the best of his/her ability in order to support the efforts of the team. The only way any member of the team can be a winner is if the entire teams wins. In sports or in business, the most notable of accomplishments lose their meaning if they are part of an overall unsuccessful team effort.

The *contributions* of each player to the team are more important than any one individual's *performance*. Often, the unsung heroes contribute the most to a team's victory. Many times the most important contributions of individuals go unnoticed — for example, the offensive lineman who opens the hole in the defense allowing the running back to score the touchdown.

1. Who are the unsung heroes on your team?

    _____
    _____
    _____
    _____
    _____

2. How could those individuals receive more recognition?

    _____
    _____
    _____
    _____
    _____
    _____
    _____

3. Does your group work as individuals or as a team?

    _____

    _____

    _____

    _____

    _____

    _____

4. How much more effectively could your work group meet its goals if you all worked more as a team than as individuals?

    _____

    _____

    _____

    _____

    _____

    _____

    _____

    _____

    _____

    _____

    _____

    _____

ACTIVITY 15

THE OPPONENT

In sports every game presents a different opponent who wants to win as much as your team does. And it is always clear who the competition is; it's the other teams you play against. However, in the world of work the opponent is not always so clear. First, you may not meet the competition face-to-face, but compete instead with others for a share of the market you all serve. The score is measured in profitability. Sometimes the competition becomes so tough that the winner eliminates the opposition, putting them out of business.

Often in your work life you do not have a clear picture of exactly who your real competition is. At times it can seem that the competition is within your organization, with one department competing against another. When departments compete with each other, they are actually helping the *real* outside competition win. Can you imagine during a football game having the offensive players tackle one another rather than blocking the defense? They would defeat themselves! You should not become your own competition. Self-directed workteams help employees view others in the organization as members of their same team.

1. A team must have a clear picture of the real competition and work together to defeat that competition. Who is your team's real competition?

    _____

    _____

    _____

    _____

    _____

    _____

    _____

    _____

    _____

    _____

    _____

2. List below the factors that currently exist in your organization that you feel could help your team defeat the competition. Then list the actions that would need to be taken to be victorious.

Factors for Winning

Actions that Need to Be Taken

_____

_____

_____

_____

_____

_____

_____

_____

_____

_____

_____

_____

_____

_____

_____

_____

_____

_____

ACTIVITY 16

GAME FILMS AND SCOUTING REPORTS

A football team studies the game films of their competition over and over again to learn as much as they can about each team. Football teams also send out scouts to watch the competition play. They report back information on both individual players' strengths and weaknesses as well as the team's general performance and strategies. From these game films and scouting reports, a team develops its own specially designed game plan for an opponent. Without game films and scouting reports, a team would have little or no information about its competition or what to expect when playing against them. The team could be planning on using the wrong strategy for an opponent, leading themselves to almost certain defeat.

A popular technique in business today is called benchmarking. Benchmarking involves comparing your organization to others that are considered to be the best in the industry. By benchmarking, an organization can set challenging new goals to remain competitive with its industry's leaders.

1. How much does your team know about your competition?

   _____

   _____

   _____

   _____

   _____

   _____

2. What would be the equivalent of game films and scouting reports that your team could use to learn more about your competition?

   _____

   _____

   _____

   _____

   _____

3.   How could learning more about your competition help your team be more successful?

_____

_____

_____

_____

_____

_____

4.   How can benchmarking make your team stronger?

_____

_____

_____

_____

_____

_____

ACTIVITY 17

KEEPING SCORE

Keeping score is important for any team to measure its performance. Imagine what sports would be like if you didn't keep score. There would be no measurement of how one team was performing as compared to another. There would be no way of knowing who was playing better or worse, or if your team was improving, or who were the winners or losers.

"How are we doing?" is a question often asked by managers and supervisors. For self-directed workteams to be successful, everyone must ask that question. Everyone must have a way of knowing how well he or she is performing his or her own job, how well the team is doing, and how well it is doing compared to the competition. In sports there is a scoreboard that tells everyone how each team is doing in the game. How do you keep score at work?

1. Where is your team's scoreboard? How is the score kept? Who keeps the score?

    _____

    _____

    _____

    _____

2. How well-informed are people at work concerning your team's score?

    _____

    _____

    _____

    _____

3. Does your team know how the competition is doing?

    _____

    _____

    _____

    _____

4. How can everyone be part of the communication process so that they will know about their team's score?

_____

_____

_____

_____

_____

_____

_____

_____

ACTIVITY 18

It is late in the fourth quarter with only two minutes to play. Your team, which is behind by four points, just regained possession of the ball on the 50-yard line. What can you do to score the winning touchdown?

Football teams train constantly for this very scenario, developing two-minute practice drills that involve a variety of "hurry up" offensive strategies designed to move against the defense in the most efficient way possible. There is a planned series of plays that they have practiced and practiced and can run without a huddle in order to save time and try to catch the other team off guard. How many football games have you watched when the last two minutes of the game determined the outcome?

Should your team at work develop and practice a two-minute drill? Are there occasions at work that require a quick response, limited time to plan your next move, or when everyone needs to have a clear understanding of what his or her role is in a critical situation?

What would be a situation at your workplace that might require a two-minute drill? Begin planning what your team's two-minute drill would include.

Your Team's Two-Minute Drill

_____

_____

_____

_____

_____

_____

_____

_____

_____

_____

_____

_____

51

ACTIVITY 19

WINNING YEAR

In most team sports a winning year occurs when a team wins more games than it loses. This is not always an easy accomplishment, particularly when you consider that in every game there are two teams, each doing its best to defeat the other. Ultimately, there are going to be winning teams and losing teams.

In the business world how do you measure winners and losers? In most cases winners are those who meet the requirements of their customers and are the most profitable. You could say that a winning season is one in which an organization reaches its profitability goals. As in football or other sports, there are other teams competing for those same goals or profits. What does it take to have a winning season? What makes the difference between a winning and a losing season?

1. How does your organization or business define "winning"?

   _____

   _____

   _____

   _____

   _____

2. What can your team do to have a winning season this year?

   _____

   _____

   _____

   _____

   _____

   _____

   _____

   _____

ACTIVITY 20

THE SUPER BOWL

Each year every football team in the NFL has as its goal to become the Super Bowl champions. Unfortunately, only one team will be able to attain this ultimate objective at the end of the season. What drives a team to overcome all of the obstacles that stand in its way to becoming a champion team?

1. What would be the equivalent of the Super Bowl for your team?

_____

_____

_____

_____

2. Are your team members committed to reaching this goal? How do you know that to be true?

_____

_____

_____

_____

_____

_____

3. What are the rewards of reaching for and winning your team's Super Bowl?

_____

_____

_____

_____

_____

_____

4. Is reaching its Super Bowl worth the effort to your team? What are the indications that the team feels this way?

_____

_____

_____

_____

_____

_____

_____

_____

ACTIVITY 21

REBUILDING YEAR

Teams sometimes have seasons when nothing goes right; when it seems the only wise thing to do is start again from the beginning. Sometimes a team must focus on what its goals are for the future rather than worry about the present season. In the sports arena this type of season typically is called a "rebuilding year." It is a time when priorities are placed on what the team should *be* rather than on what the team *is*. In sports a rebuilding year may involve giving younger players some important playing experience, changing game strategies, retraining players to perform different positions and so on.

1. If this is a rebuilding year for your team, what would you as the coach expect to accomplish to help make your team stronger for the future?

   _____

   _____

   _____

   _____

2. What would you set as the short-term priorities for the team?

   _____

   _____

   _____

   _____

   _____

3. What long-term priorities would you set for the team?

   _____

   _____

   _____

   _____

   _____

PART FIVE

COACHING A WINNING TEAM

There is an old saying in professional football: "On any given Sunday any team can beat any other team." Not only is this true in the NFL, but it is true in almost any kind of competition. How many times each season are there major upsets, when a team that no one expected to come even close to winning is victorious despite the odds against it? How can this happen? The reasons may be many, but the single most important factor is ATTITUDE.

A winning attitude can overcome many adversities both in sports and in business. A team will not remain on top for very long without a winning attitude. Attitude is what enables the underdog team to defeat the champions. A winning attitude means having pride in your work and the desire to do your very best for both your team and yourself. Many times the success of a team is not a question of how much money is spent but of how determined the players are. Victory often comes to the team that wants it most.

Through increased responsibility and involvement, self-directed workteams can dramatically change people's attitudes about their jobs. This usually translates into everyone feeling more a part of the team and having a greater committment to be successful.

Now turn to the following pages and complete Activities 22 through 31.

ACTIVITY 22

WINNING ATTITUDE

1. What makes a team have a winning attitude?

    _____
    _____
    _____
    _____
    _____

2. What kind of attitude does your team have? How is it expressed by the team?

    _____
    _____
    _____
    _____
    _____

3. What can you do as coach of your team to help the members develop or maintain a winning attitude?

    _____
    _____
    _____
    _____
    _____
    _____
    _____
    _____

ACTIVITY 23

THE WALLS

At many places of work, "walls" exist that prevent people at different levels of the organization from working together as a team or from even communicating effectively with one another. These walls are extremely difficult to tear down, particularly when they have existed for many years. What makes these walls even more difficult to eliminate is the fact that they are imaginary and are created by people's attitudes. These walls traditionally have defined each employee's job and scope of responsibility. As part of this definition, these walls have represented attitudes such as, "You worry about your job and I'll worry about mine" or, "My problems do not go beyond the boundaries of my walls!"

In today's changing workplace it is mandatory that these walls be torn down. No longer can these boundaries exist, boundaries that limit people's ability to share their knowledge, experience, and expertise in an effort to help their organization move forward. "That's not my problem" is not a true statement if that problem has the potential to have an impact on any part of the organization.

1. Where do imaginary walls exist in your organization? What would these walls be called?

_____

_____

_____

_____

_____

2. How can these walls be torn down so that they cannot be rebuilt in the future?

_____

_____

_____

_____

_____

_____

ACTIVITY 24

There is a contest that has been going on as long as people have worked to earn their own living. It is call "We vs. They." The "we" represents the employees' views of themselves regardless of the organizational level. "They" represents everyone else in the organization. To management "they" are the workers; to the workers "they" means the management. Typically no one knows who "they" really are, as no one wants to admit that they are part of the problem. "They" are usually blamed for anything that goes wrong in the organization, and in reality they often actually are the cause. "We" frequently know what "they" should have done. If only "we" had been asked, we could have saved "them" a great deal of time and money — not to mention frustration.

The problem is that "we" and "they" are not supposed to be on opposing sides — everyone should be on the same team. The things that "we" know should be shared with "them." "They" need to give everyone a chance to share their knowledge and experience for the benefit of all concerned.

Achieving an "us" attitude is the goal of self-directed workteams. Organizations no longer can afford to compete within themselves. Everyone at all levels needs to view the organization as representing "us" rather than "we vs. they." Working together rather than working divided is the key to success for any team.

Do you have a "we vs. they" attitude in your organization? If so, what steps could be taken to begin to change that attitude?

_____

_____

_____

_____

_____

_____

_____

_____

_____

_____

ACTIVITY 25

MOVING IN THE SAME DIRECTION

It is a simple fact that two equal forces moving in opposite directions will stand still as one force cancels out the other. However, if these forces combine rather than compete, they have more than twice the force they have separately. This basic concept applies to organizations as well as to sports teams.

How much energy and how many resources do you think most team members expend by not working together, or in other words by moving in opposite directions? What happens as a result of all this energy being wasted, and what is the cost both personally and to the organization? The more that team members fight or compete among themselves, the more they actually help their competition, because they are wasting the potential strength of their own team. The competition is tough enough out there without helping them to defeat you. The members of a team need to move in the same direction if they are to reach the team's goals.

How strong is your team? What might be the potential of your team if more effort were expended in pulling together rather than competing with each other?

_____

_____

_____

_____

_____

_____

_____

_____

_____

_____

_____

_____

_____

_____

_____

ACTIVITY 26

OUT OF THE BLEACHERS AND ONTO THE FIELD

You might ask, "Why should I care what happens in other parts of the organization or company that I work for; all I'm concerned about is my job and what I'm responsible for!" But, not being concerned about what happens outside the scope of your job could eventually mean no longer having a job. Each person who works for a company or organization must actively contribute as a member of the team for the benefit of everyone on the team.

Too often people sit in the bleachers and watch others play the game. It is easy to sit in the stands and criticize how the game is being played. It is a different game when you are on the field playing in it. By getting off the bleachers, members of self-directed workteams gain a better understanding for and appreciation of what is involved in solving problems in the workplace. When self-directed workteams are introduced, you often hear comments such as: "I never realized just how difficult it is to make changes in our organization until I became involved with a self-directed workteam. Problems aren't as easy to solve as they look when you're just sitting back and watching."

The more players in the game, the stronger the team. Imagine how tough a football team would be if everyone on the team could be on the field at the same time. Unlike most sports, the number of active players on *your* team who can play in the game at the same time has no limit as you work together to beat the competition.

Do you have more spectators than players on your team? If so, what is the single most important thing you could do to get more players on the field?

_____

_____

_____

_____

_____

_____

_____

_____

_____

ACTIVITY 27

WHAT CAN I DO ABOUT IT?

"I" is a very big word. "I" is where everything begins. People often ask, "What can I do about it, I'm only one person?" The fact is that you can do a lot about almost anything. When you think about it, "I" is one of the few things over which an individual has complete control. Everything else can only be influenced indirectly. Each of us makes the decisions about what we say, do, or think. There is no limit to what a single individual can accomplish when he or she is determined and committed to reach a particular goal.

Any kind of team consists of individuals. What makes those individuals a team is when they work together toward achieving shared goals. A team can accomplish much more than any one individual. With all of the team members working together, the result is much greater than just the sum of the individual efforts. In other words, two plus two equals more than four. This super achievement is called *synergy*. Synergy is one of the most needed elements in any team or organization, and it begins with each player's individual contribution to the team.

1. Do you think your team works together in such a way that the results are more than a simple collection of the team members' efforts? If not, what do you think is preventing peak results?

_____

_____

_____

_____

_____

_____

_____

_____

_____

_____

_____

_____

_____

_____

2. What might be done to help the team members work more effectively together?

_____

_____

_____

_____

_____

_____

_____

_____

_____

_____

_____

_____

_____

_____

_____

_____

ACTIVITY 28

OWNERSHIP

When you own something, it belongs to you. You take special care of that which you own to ensure that it keeps its value and lasts for many years. This same concept also applies to your job. To have a sense of ownership of your job, you must feel that it belongs to you and that you have the responsibility for its success. To create this sense of ownership, the organization must give you sufficient opportunities to make the important decisions that affect your job and make you accountable for the results of your decisions, regardless of the outcome. Ownership also creates a desire to increase the value of what you own. Self-directed workteams help employees search for ways to increase the value of their jobs both for themselves and for the organization.

Having a sense of ownership can be compared to renting. Renters have a completely different level of commitment than do homeowners. The concept of job ownership is extremely important to the success of self-directed work-teams. Employees in every sense of the word need to assume ownership of their jobs. In doing so they must also accept the responsibilities that accompany ownership. As opposed to renting, which involves simply using something for a period of time to serve a temporary need and then leaving it or giving it back, ownership requires a long-term commitment.

This same sense of ownership needs to be felt by each employee in regard to the total organization. Each employee must view the organization as if it belonged to him or her. Self-directed workteams, through increased involvement and commitment, help create a greater sense of ownership for employees at all levels of the organization.

1. If you owned the company, how would you feel about customers not being served to their satisfaction, or about materials being wasted unnecessarily?

_____

_____

_____

_____

_____

_____

_____

2. Would you perform your job differently than you are performing right now? In what way(s)?

_____

_____

_____

_____

_____

_____

_____

_____

3. How can you help your team members to feel a greater sense of ownership in their work?

_____

_____

_____

_____

_____

_____

_____

_____

_____

ACTIVITY 29

SUPERSTARS

On most teams certain players stand out among their teammates because of their distinguished abilities and performances. Often these players are called stars or even superstars. Superstars can be exciting to watch, and they make a tremendous difference in the success of a team. They receive a great deal of attention and publicity, and in professional sports they usually receive incredible salaries. However, sometimes all this attention and big salaries can cause resentment among the other players who make only a fraction of the superstar's big contract and work just as hard, with little or no recognition.

1. Who are the superstars on your team?

_____

_____

_____

2. What influence do they have on the other members of your team?

_____

_____

_____

_____

_____

3. Is it possible for every player to be a star or superstar? How?

_____

_____

_____

_____

_____

_____

_____

ACTIVITY 30

WORK VS. PLAY

What is the difference between work and play? Most people probably would answer that play is fun and work is not. But why? What makes play fun and work seem like "work"? Consider the following example of a typical leisure activity that many people enjoy as a way to relax and unwind after working hard at their jobs.

This activity is performed by each of the members of a team working toward the objective of beating their competition. As members of this team, the players must take their turn trying to strike a small, round object thrown at them in a manner intended to make this task extremely difficult to accomplish. The players use a long cylindrical device to attempt to project this moving round object in the opposite direction. The player gets a limited number of attempts to complete this assignment. If unsuccessful, the entire team is penalized and the player must relinquish his or her turn to the next player, who hopefully will be more successful. It should also be noted that while attempting to accomplish this task, members of the other team and their supporters may be yelling encouraging messages to their own team and may even say impolite things about members of the opposing team as it attempts to perform its duties. When the object is struck, the player must run as fast as he or she can to the first of four designated stops on the playing area. The player can advance to the next stop only under very specific circumstances. Under these circumstances the player must again run as fast as he or she can to get to the next stop. During all of this action there are nine players on the opposing team doing everything they can to prevent the player from being able to advance to the next designated location. There are very specific rules governing all of these activities. Each team must take turns trading duties and responsibilities throughout the contest. At the end of this activity, there will be a winner and a loser.

Why do people enjoy this activity? Why do they find it more enjoyable than work? No doubt they find it challenging and personally rewarding. They enjoy working as a member of a team with each player making his or her contribution toward the team's success. They enjoy the support and reinforcement the players provide by complimenting one another on their good performance and offering them encouragement when they are less successful. They enjoy the support they receive from the team's fans who take an active interest in the team, cheering the team on game after game. They enjoy feeling a sense of accomplishment with each victory they celebrate together. Sometimes the team's accomplishments are publicized throughout the community so that everyone learns of the team's successes.

Why can't the same factors that allow people to enjoy playing baseball, softball, or other team sports be present at work? The answer is that they *can* be with the help of self-directed workteams. Self-directed workteams add fun to work, making it more rewarding and satisfying for everyone. As one member of such a workteam said, "Being on a self-directed workteam has brought the fun back to work again. I am once again looking forward to going to work. Every day is a new challenge, and I enjoy working together as part of a team."

What factors could be enhanced or added to your current work situation to make the job more fun, rewarding, and satisfying for everyone?

_____

_____

_____

_____

_____

_____

_____

_____

_____

_____

_____

_____

_____

_____

_____

_____

_____

_____

_____

_____

_____

_____

ACTIVITY 31

THE LOCKER ROOM

The locker room — that famous place where the coach gives his emotional half-time speech, which inspires and motivates his players to rally together to come from behind to win the big game for the gipper; the scene of jubilant victory celebrations or a solemn sanctuary of defeat. In either case the locker room provides a meeting place for the team to communicate with one another and to focus on the game.

1. Where is your team's "locker room" or meeting place, and how effectively do you as the coach use it to communicate with your players?

    _____

    _____

    _____

    _____

    _____

2. What should you say to your team before the "big game," or the equivalent in your organization, to help motivate them to be winners?

    _____

    _____

    _____

    _____

    _____

    _____

    _____

    _____

    _____

    _____

    _____

3. Let's say it's half-time of a big game, and your team is behind. What would be your half-time speech to your team, as it applies to the game (business/service) your team plays?

Your Half-Time Speech

_____

_____

_____

_____

_____

_____

_____

_____

_____

_____

_____

_____

_____

_____

_____

_____

_____

_____

_____

_____

_____

_____

_____

_____

_____

_____

_____

PART SIX

GAME PLAY

You now have your players, your team, and you have learned the basic fundamentals of the game. As coach, you have helped develop your employees to become a self-directed workteam, with each player striving to reach his or her shared team goal of being a champion in your business. You have practiced hard and are ready to play in the big game.

ACTIVITY 32

THE HUDDLE

The way people communicate can either cause or solve many of the problems they have when working together. In other words, communication can be a liability or a strength, depending on how effectively you communicate. If your work group were a football team, would eleven players stand around arguing about what the next play should be until the team is penalized for delaying the game? Or, would you have a game plan and huddle before each play so that everyone knows his or her roles and responsibilities?

In football the quarterback huddles with the team before each play to communicate the play to execute next. Regardless of whose decision it is to run the play, each player must have a clear understanding of what his role and responsibilities are for the particular play that is called. Imagine how confusing a football game would be without the huddle, with no one knowing for sure what his responsibilities and roles will be for the team's next play. How often in the workplace do we try to "run a play" without all the players understanding what is expected of them and what the direction and plan are for the team?

Have you ever tried to take a shortcut by giving hurried instructions to your employees concerning a job they were to perform, only to end up needing to take more time later on to adequately explain the task to them? When was the last time you had a "huddle" with your team? Perhaps having a huddle before each "play" to communicate the game plan, roles, and responsibilities for everyone on the team is not only a good idea in football but in the workplace as well!

How often do you take the time to huddle with your team? Recall a situation when you didn't take time to plan adequately with your team. What happened as a result?

_____

_____

_____

_____

_____

_____

_____

ACTIVITY 33

As any football team begins to look forward to playing the game, thought must be given to the defenses it will face. At your workplace, the competition intends to prevent your team from reaching its goal or even to move your team in the opposite direction. The competition would like nothing more than to take the ball from your team and return it to its own goal line.

Imagine that the opposition's defense represents the obstacles that exist between your team and your goals. Are any of the following suggested defenses/obstacles examples of those your team must overcome? Put a check mark by those that apply.

_____ Poor communications

_____ Low moral

_____ Changing technology

_____ Costs

_____ Down-time

_____ Customer complaints

_____ Defects

_____ Price

_____ Market share

_____ Economy

_____ Regulations

List other obstacles that block your team from reaching its goals.

_____

_____

_____

_____

_____

_____

ACTIVITY 34

THE OFFENSE

Every football team must have an offense designed to overcome the defense's efforts to stop its forward progress. Each offensive position has specific responsibilities for dealing with some aspect of the defense. Many of these responsibilities, such as opening holes in the defense or providing pass protection, involve making it possible for other players to perform their jobs. If everyone does his/her job and supports one another, the offense will succeed. In football a team has no direct control over its opponent's defense. A team can only affect the other team's defense through the actions of its own offense. This operating principle is true for your team at work as well.

As noted earlier, poor communication often poses a major obstacle that a team must overcome (defeat) to reach its goal. Let's use this as an example and put it onto a football playing field. We will use the football game to show how problems/obstacles might be tackled. On your "Self-Directed Playing Field" on the next page, you will see that **Poor Communication** has been lined up as your opponent's defense.

The Self-Directed Playing Field

Reaching Your Team's Goals

G -

10 -

20 -

**D
E
F
E
N
S
E**

30 -

40 -

Poor Communication

50 -

40 -

30 -

**O
F
F
E
N
S
E**

20 -

10 -

G -

Moving Away from Your Team's Goals

Getting Ready to Play

What can you do to overcome the opposition's defense, as represented by **Poor Communication**? Look at the Self-Directed Playing Field on page 89. For this example, your offensive team has been lined up against the defense. Some of your "players" against **Poor Communication** are: Customer Feedback, Open Door Policy, Weekly Team Meetings, etc.

The Self-Directed Playing Field

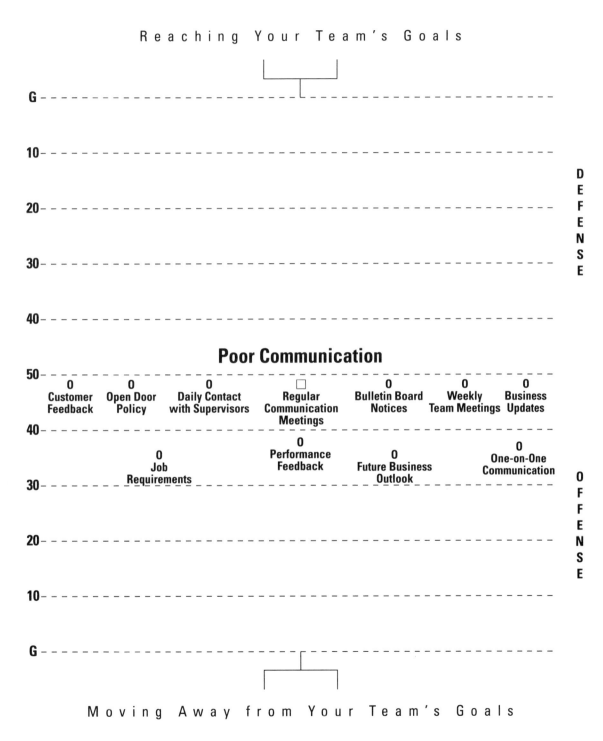

Reaching Your Team's Goals

G

10

20

30

40

DEFENSE

Poor Communication

50

0 Customer Feedback

0 Open Door Policy

0 Daily Contact with Supervisors

□ Regular Communication Meetings

0 Bulletin Board Notices

0 Weekly Team Meetings

0 Business Updates

40

0 Job Requirements

0 Performance Feedback

0 Future Business Outlook

0 One-on-One Communication

30

OFFENSE

20

10

G

Moving Away from Your Team's Goals

Play Action

We will use this football example to defeat one of your obstacles/defenses. Begin by selecting one of the obstacles you listed in Activity 33. Place that obstacle in the defensive position on the blank playing field on page 92.

Now establish your offensive team. That is, what are some actions you can take to beat your obstacle? Refer to the offensive lineup on the example field: customer feedback, weekly team meetings, etc., are some of the offensive players against the defense, **Poor Communication**. Put your offensive line up against your obstacle/defense on the same blank playing field. (Two additional blank playing fields have been supplied for use with different obstacles.)

As we go back to our example, the offensive team scores a big touchdown against the defense — **Poor Communication**. See how this is done by looking at the example on the next page. In this pass play, the offensive line, consisting of *Open Door Policy*, *Daily Contact with Supervisors*, *Regular Communications Meetings*, *Bulletin Board Notices*, and *Weekly Team Meetings* provides pass protection as quarterback, *Performance Feedback*, fakes a handoff to halfback, *Future Business Outlook*, who goes up the middle. The other halfback, *Job Requirements*, also provides pass protection as *Performance Feedback* drops back into the pocket to pass. Split end, *Customer Feedback*, and flanker, *One-on-One Communication*, go downfield and run their pass patterns. *Performance Feedback* finds *One-on-One Communication* open in the end zone and connects for a touchdown!

After developing your offenses, begin drawing your own plays to lead your team to victory!

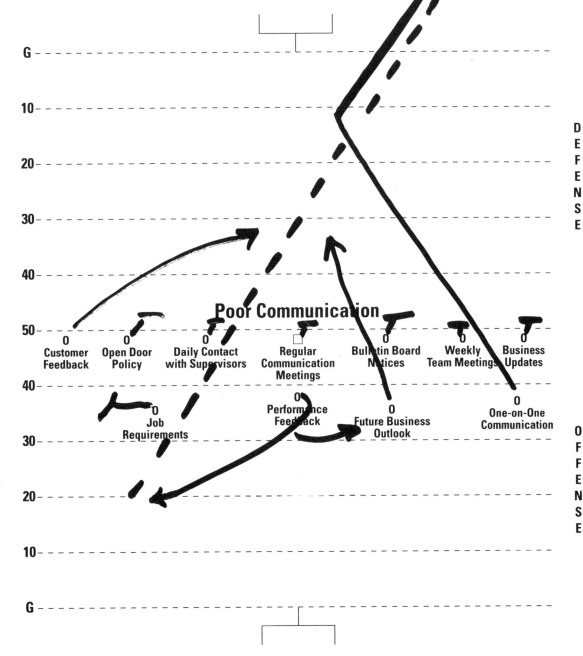

The Self-Directed Playing Field

Touchdown

Reaching Your Team's Goals

G

10

20

30

40

DEFENSE

Poor Communication

50

Customer
Feedback

Open Door
Policy

Daily Contact
with Supervisors

Regular
Communication
Meetings

Bulletin Board
Notices

Weekly
Team Meetings

Business
Updates

40

Job
Requirements

Performance
Feedback

Future Business
Outlook

One-on-One
Communication

30

OFFENSE

20

10

G

Moving Away from Your Team's Goals

The Self-Directed Playing Field

Reaching Your Team's Goals

G -

10 -

20 -

30 -

40 -

50 -

40 -

30 -

20 -

10 -

G -

Moving Away from Your Team's Goals

The Self-Directed Playing Field

Reaching Your Team's Goals

G -

10 -

20 -   **D**
                                                       E

30 -   **F**
    E

40 -   **N**

50 -   **S**

40 -   **E**

30 -   **O**

20 -   **F**
   F

10 -   **E**
   N

G -   **S**
   E

Moving Away from Your Team's Goals

The Self-Directed Playing Field

Reaching Your Team's Goals

G –

10 –

20 –

30 –

40 –

50 –

40 –

30 –

20 –

10 –

G –

Moving Away from Your Team's Goals

D
E
F
E
N
S
E

O
F
F
E
N
S
E

ACTIVITY 35

FUMBLES/TURNOVERS

Fumbles and turnovers are part of the game. However, for the team losing the ball, turnovers can be costly mistakes. Turnovers not only end a team's forward drive to the goal line, they also give the ball to the opposition! It also is emotionally defeating for a team to see its progress handed over to the other team.

There are fumbles and turnovers at work as well. How does a business or organization lose the ball to the competition? How costly can a fumble or turnover be to your team? How can your team prevent fumbles or turnovers from happening?

1. List some of the possible fumbles your organization has made or might make.

    _____

    _____

    _____

    _____

2. What might be done to prevent past fumbles from happening in the future?

    _____

    _____

    _____

    _____

3. How might your team members be more involved in preventing these fumbles and turnovers?

    _____

    _____

    _____

    _____

ACTIVITY 36

THE WRONG CALL

Typically on many football teams the coach calls the plays for the offense to run by sending in a play with a player or signaling the quarterback from the sidelines. Imagine then during the huddle as the quarterback is about to call the coach's pass play, the offensive right tackle says, "I can open a hole in the defense wide enough to drive a truck through. Call our off-tackle running play and we'll score a touchdown for sure!" The quarterback looks at the faces of the other players in the huddle and sees that everyone agrees with the tackle. The other team has covered the pass receivers heavily all day, essentially shutting down their passing game. The quarterback must make a decision quickly before being penalized for delay of game. The team is behind by six points, it is late in the fourth quarter, and third down with no time-outs remaining. Most likely this is the team's last chance to come from behind to win. What would you do if you were the quarterback?

This situation represents what self-directed workteams are all about — giving those people in the organization who are in the best positions to "call the plays" an opportunity not only to be heard but listened to. Too many times in the past, organizations have not utilized their most valuable asset — the employees — in making decisions that potentially affect everyone's success and future. Too often the management group has called the wrong play when the right call was clear to others working closer to the action. Frequently the answers to problems are found simply by asking the right people for their input.

Do the coaches in your organization call all the plays, or are the players called on for their input? What changes could be made in the way you are currently utilizing your employees?

_____

_____

_____

_____

_____

_____

_____

_____

ACTIVITY 37

PENALTIES

Penalties are part of the game of football as well as other sports. Referees charge penalties against a team for breaking the rules of the game. Penalties in football can cost the offense valuable yards, cause the loss of first down opportunities, and even cancel out touchdowns, extra points, and field goals. Defensive penalties give away hard fought yards to the other team's offense. Penalties can turn a great play into a fruitless effort. One person's mistake can take away another player's achievements. Penalties can and often do make the difference in the final outcome of any game.

1. What are some of the possible penalties for making mistakes or not following the rules of the "game" that your team plays at work?

   _____

   _____

   _____

   _____

2. What are the consequences of those penalties? Could those penalties make your team less successful or cause you to lose the game?

   _____

   _____

   _____

   _____

3. How can those penalties be avoided in the future?

   _____

   _____

   _____

   _____

ACTIVITY 38

INJURIES

A sports injury can keep an athlete out of next week's big game, the rest of the season, or even end his or her career. While injuries are part of every game, many things may be done to prevent them from occurring. Injuries can devastate an employee just as they can an athlete. An injury can take an employee out of the "game" for days, weeks, months, or even end a career.

1. What can a sports coach, a workplace coach, and the team members do to prevent injuries to their players?

    Sports Coach

    _____

    _____

    _____

    _____

    _____

    Workplace Coach

    _____

    _____

    _____

    _____

    _____

    Team Members

    _____

    _____

    _____

    _____

    _____

2.   What are the actions that are common to all three?

_____

_____

_____

_____

_____

_____

3.   Develop your own plan to prevent injuries to your team members.

_____

_____

_____

_____

_____

_____

_____

_____

_____

_____

_____

_____

_____

_____

_____

_____

_____

_____

_____

_____

ACTIVITY 39

VICTORY CELEBRATIONS

Nothing is more rewarding to a team than to be victorious. In victory a team celebrates what it has accomplished with all of its members working together. For that moment when the final gun sounds and a team has defeated the competition, there is no greater feeling of teamwork. Soon the team members must look ahead to the next week's challenge, but for today they are winners!

1. How does your team celebrate its "victories"?

_____

_____

_____

_____

_____

_____

_____

2. How can celebrating its victories help your team continue to be winners?

_____

_____

_____

_____

_____

_____

_____

_____

_____

_____

Everyone a Champion

Regardless of the game, certain criteria measure the success of any team, for example, reaching the playoffs or becoming the champions. However, there are other criteria that measure success as well, that are perhaps even more important. These may include the feeling of teamwork among the players, the pride they have in their team, the support of their fans, or their shared sense of accomplishment that comes from achieving what they have worked on together. Perhaps these factors, more than any others, are the real measures of success for a team.

What does it take to be a champion, and what motivates players to reach this ultimate goal? Support, recognition, respect, and appreciation are just a few of the motivators that drive people to want to do their very best — to strive to reach goals that they may otherwise have thought unattainable. It is important for any team or individual to feel like a champion. As a coach, perhaps your most important job is to treat your players and your team like champions.

The self-directed workteam is not a new concept, particularly as it relates to roles such as coach or supervisor; only the terminology is new. Coaches, supervisors, and others in leadership positions have always needed to be self-directed. They always have had to make decisions for themselves and accept responsibility. That is the nature of their jobs. What is changing today are the organizations in which we work. The supervisors' role today is to help others within their organizations accept the same or similar level of responsibility and commitment that the supervisors have accepted in their jobs. Everyone on the team has the potential to be a star or even a superstar. In the new role of coach, each supervisor must give each individual the opportunity to shine.

Instant Replay

- The competition gets tougher every day.

- You can be better tomorrow than you are today.

- Every job is important to the success of the team.

- Everyone must be included in the team's "huddle."

- Every player must share in the responsibility for the success of the team.

- Every player can be a superstar.

- Every team can be the champion.

PART SEVEN

POST GAME REPORT

After a big game has been played usually there is a *Post Game Report* that wraps up all of the important plays and events leading to the final outcome. What is your Post Game Report for your performance as a Coach? How can you improve your team's performance in the future? How can you improve your performance?

A football team must examine its weakest points and develop plans for improving them before its next game. In which of the following activities would you consider yourself the weakest? Check all that apply.

_____ Activity 1:   Your Role as a Supervisor

_____ Activity 2:   The Effects of Confidence

_____ Activity 3:   The Greatest Coach

_____ Activity 4:   The Team Owner

_____ Activity 5:   The Fans

_____ Activity 6:   Community Support

_____ Activity 7:   Publicity

_____ Activity 8:   Monday Morning Quarterback

_____ Activity 9:   Bench Strength

_____ Activity 10:   The Basics of the Game

_____ Activity 11:   Playbook

_____ Activity 12:   Game Plan

_____ Activity 13:   Goals

_____ Activity 14:   Unsung Heros

_____ Activity 15:   The Opponent

_____ Activity 16:   Game Films and Scouting Reports

_____ Activity 17:   Keeping Score

_____ Activity 18:   The Two-Minute Drill

_____ Activity 19:   Winning Year

_____ Activity 20:   The Super Bowl

_____ Activity 21:   Rebuilding Year

_____ Activity 22:   Winning Attitude

_____ Activity 23:   The Walls

_____ Activity 24:   We vs. They

_____ Activity 25:   Moving in the Same Direction

_____ Activity 26:   Out of the Bleachers and onto the Field

_____ Activity 27:   What Can I Do about It?

_____ Activity 28:   Ownership

_____ Activity 29:   Superstars

_____ Activity 30:   Work vs. Play

_____ Activity 31:   The Locker Room

_____ Activity 32:   The Huddle

_____ Activity 33:   The Defense

_____ Activity 34:   The Offense

_____ Activity 35:   Fumbles/Turnovers

_____ Activity 36:   The Wrong Call

_____ Activity 37:   Penalties

_____ Activity 38:   Injuries

_____ Activity 39:   Victory Celebrations

Now, go back and review each of those activities/areas you identified as needing improvement and develop a "Game Plan" for turning those weaknesses into strengths. You *can* coach your self-directed workteam to victory!

Your Game Plan

_____

_____

_____

_____

_____

_____

_____

_____

_____

_____

_____

_____

_____

_____

_____

_____

_____

_____

_____

_____

_____

_____

_____

_____

_____

_____

_____

_____

·